My Life as a Victorian Maid

The Victorians	2
Up with the Lark	4
Look Smart	6
Good Job?	8
Dirty Slops	10
Wake the Family	12
Breakfast Time	14
Say Your Prayers	16
Morning Slog	18
Grab Lunch	20
Quick Rest	22
Dinner Party	24
Time Out	26
Off to Bed	28
Could you Survive as a Victorian Maid?	30
Glossary and Index	32

Written by Deborah Chancellor

Illustrated by Jez Tuya

The Victorians

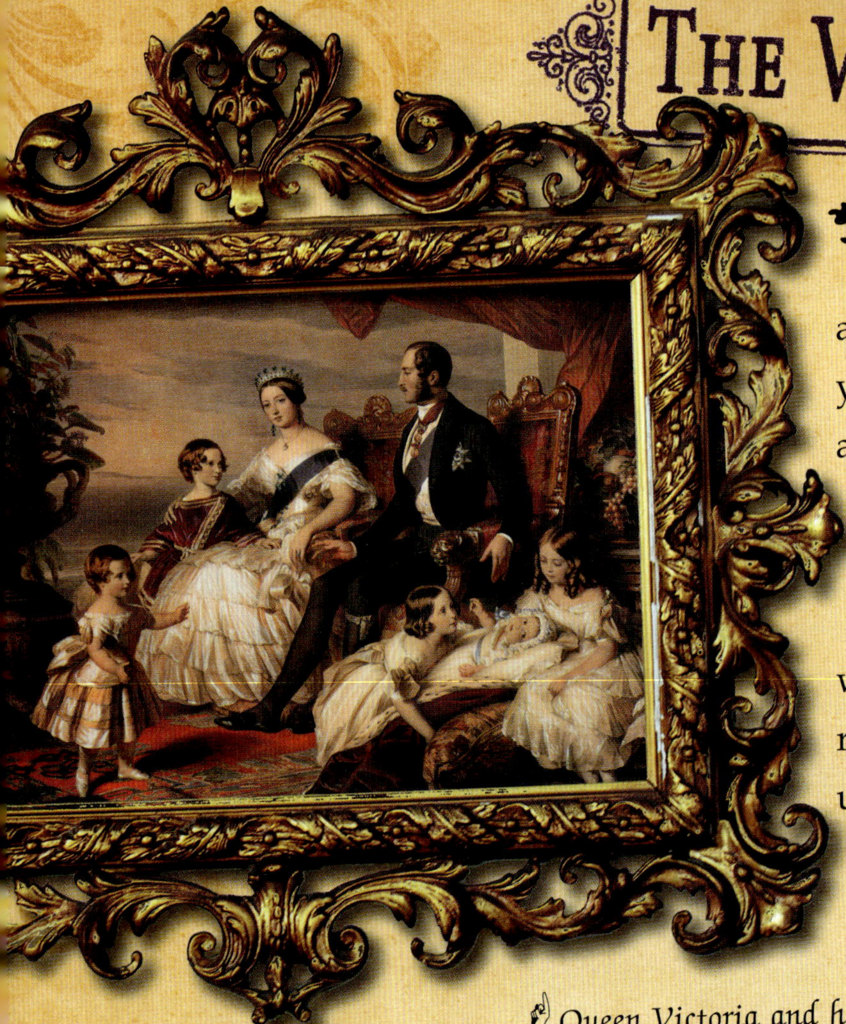

If you were born in Britain a hundred and fifty years ago, you would have been a Victorian. Queen Victoria was Queen of Great Britain and Ireland at that time. She was crowned in 1837 and ruled for sixty-four years, until she died in 1901.

Queen Victoria and her husband Prince Albert had nine children. Here are five of them.

Life in Victorian times

Life would be very different for you if you were a Victorian – there were no TVs, no internet, no smart phones! If you were poor, you would have to work hard for a living. Many poor children were servants in rich Victorian households. It wasn't an easy life!

Victorians in history

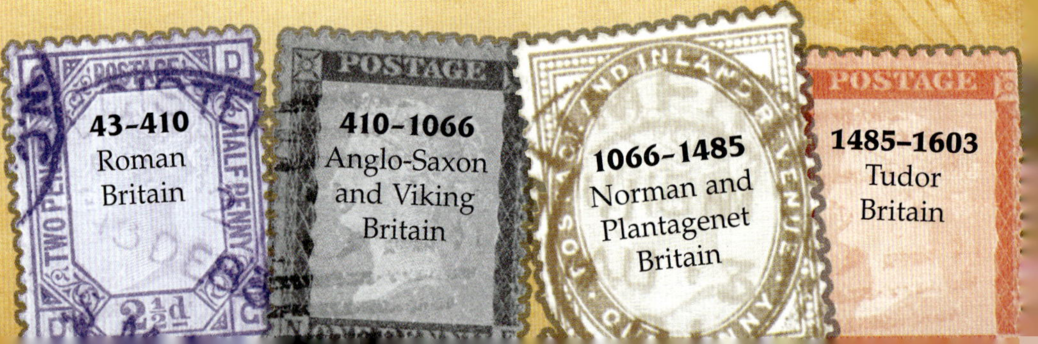

43–410 Roman Britain

410–1066 Anglo-Saxon and Viking Britain

1066–1485 Norman and Plantagenet Britain

1485–1603 Tudor Britain

Time of change

During the Victorian age, many people moved from the country to live in towns and cities. The kinds of jobs children did changed – they swapped outdoor farm labour for work in factories, workshops and mines.

If I were a Victorian, I'd want to be rich! Then I'd have enough to eat, and I'd get an education and not have to work.

DID YOU KNOW?

Incredible inventions
Did you know the camera, bike, telephone and flushing toilet were all Victorian inventions? The Victorians also made many medical discoveries, such as **antiseptic**.

The first Victorian bike was called the penny farthing.

1603–1714 Stuart Britain

1714–1837 Georgian Britain

1837–1901 Victorian Britain

1901–1918 Edwardian Britain and World War I

1920–1945 The Twenties, Thirties and World War II

Up with the Lark

Early bird

Are you always first to get up in the morning? Or do you like to snuggle back under the duvet? Imagine you are a maid in a big Victorian house, a hundred and fifty years ago. You are 12 years old and are serving a rich family. It is hard work. You have to get up at 5 a.m. every day, to start on your long list of chores. Doesn't sound like fun, does it?

DID YOU KNOW?

Up in the attic

Maids slept in tiny rooms up in the attic. There was no space for toys or books – but maids didn't have much spare time anyway. It would have been cold, and there was no electricity.

Two or more maids often had to share a room.

Creature comforts

Once a maid had dragged herself out of bed, there was no time to lose. She poured cold water from a jug into a bowl and splashed it on her face. Then she pulled on her uniform and carried her **chamber pot** downstairs. She would not have had the luxury of a hot shower or flushing toilet.

> I always enjoy my long shower in the morning - I'm so glad I have hot water!

THINK ABOUT IT!

GOING HOME
Imagine not getting to see your family every day. Victorian maids hardly ever went home. When they did, they would have to walk many miles to get there as they could not afford the fare on an **omnibus** or steam train. A maid's family would often live in a tiny, overcrowded cottage — very different from the grand house where she worked.

Victorian maids came from poor homes.

Look Smart

Dress to impress

Do you moan about your school uniform? Be grateful you didn't have to save up your pocket money to buy it. A maid had to look very smart. When she started working for a family, she would be given a uniform to wear – but it wasn't always free. It could take her two years to pay back her employers for her uniform. She only earned £7 a year!

Stand tall

A maid usually wore a long black dress with a stiff white collar and an apron to keep her dress clean. She tucked her hair into a white cap with lace trimmings. Her polished boots had to be comfortable, because she was on her feet all day. No chance of a trendy pair of shoes!

I thought my school uniform was bad until I saw what those poor Victorian maids had to wear!

A Victorian maid would lose her job if she looked scruffy.

THINK ABOUT IT!

WHAT TO WEAR?

Imagine having to wear your parents' old clothes. Children from poor families wore old adult cast-offs that were cut down to fit. Upper-class Victorian children had a better deal. They dressed in small versions of the latest adult fashions. Girls wore long dresses and boys wore tailored suits.

Rich Victorian children had beautiful, expensive clothes.

Dear Diary,
Day one in service – so much to remember! Some rules I've learned so far:

- Speak only when spoken to and never give opinions

- Only say 'good morning' or 'goodnight' if someone else says it first

- Answer to 'Mary' – all maids are called that round here

- Tie back hair – last maid was sacked because of her long fringe

Good Job?

Take your pick

If you were a poor Victorian child, you would have to go out to work from an early age. Girls were lucky because from 8 years of age they could become servants for rich families. Believe it or not, that was one of the best jobs you could get. Look at what else was on offer!

Before 1874, anyone was allowed to work in a factory, even children under 10 years old.

FACTORY WORKER

Start from 5 years of age! Work up to sixteen hours a day!

Job description
✝ Do boring, repetitive tasks all day
✝ Work very long shifts without proper breaks
✝ Clean under machines while they are still running

Possible hazards
✝ Lose a finger, hand or foot in an accident
✝ Burn yourself on hot machinery
✝ Get ill from factory pollution
✝ Go deaf from factory noise

MINER

Start from 3 years of age!

Job description
✝ Open and shut doors to let air through tunnels
✝ Push coal trucks underground
✝ Start work before dawn and never see daylight

Possible hazards
✝ Be poisoned by gas or killed in an explosion
✝ Get crushed in a rock fall
✝ Become sick from breathing coal dust

CHIMNEY SWEEP

Boys only!

Job description
✝ Start when you are five or six years old
✝ Climb up chimneys in big houses
✝ Scrape the soot out of chimney pipes

Possible hazards
✝ Get stuck in a narrow pipe and suffocate
✝ Burn in a chimney fire
✝ Get ill from breathing in soot all day

🖎 In 1875, a law was passed to stop boys from working as chimney sweeps.

Dirty Slops

Nice work

What do you have to do before you go to school every day? However busy you are, you can be sure a Victorian maid was busier! At 6 a.m., a maid had to go into the kitchen to boil water for the family to wash with. The house was chilly, so she would hurry from room to room, lighting the fires in the fireplaces. At 6.45 a.m., it would be time for her 'favourite' job of all – emptying the chamber pots. Imagine having to do that!

Some posh Victorian chamber pots were beautifully decorated.

DID YOU KNOW?

Fire alarm

A Victorian maid had to be very careful with fire. If she dropped a candle, she could set fire to her skirt. One spark from a fireplace could burn the house down.

Toilet trouble

In the 1880s, if you had a flushing toilet, everyone knew you were rich! Even so, people didn't always use them at night. Why bother, if your maid would empty your chamber pot every morning? Things were not quite so easy for poor Victorian families. A crowded city street would have just one or two outside toilets for everyone to use, called **privies**. Would you like sharing a toilet with all your neighbours?

Privies were draughty wooden sheds. Some had wooden seats like this, but some were just holes in the ground!

THINK ABOUT IT!

FILTHY DIRTY

Living conditions in Victorian cities were terrible and drinking water was dirty. Sewage flowed through the streets and millions died from killer diseases that were spread by the polluted water, such as cholera and dysentery. By 1866, a network of sewers was built under the streets of London. Soon the health of the people who lived there began to improve.

WAKE THE FAMILY

Morning call

By 7 a.m., a maid would have been up for two hours. It was time for the master's children to eat, so the maid would take a breakfast tray to the nursery. The children might have toast and eggs. This would smell amazing – but the maid wouldn't be able to eat anything herself for another hour. At 7.30 a.m., she would take a tray with morning tea up to her master and mistress.

Perambulators (prams) were invented in about 1850. They were so expensive only rich families could afford them.

THINK ABOUT IT!

OUT OF SIGHT

Imagine having to keep out of the way of your parents for most of the day. A rich Victorian child had no choice. You were looked after by a nanny in the nursery. This was where you ate, played and had lessons. Victorian parents did not talk much to their children and expected them to 'be seen and not heard'.

Know your place

After the maid had returned to the kitchen with her empty trays, she would set the table for the servants' breakfast. Maids were among the least important servants, so they had to serve the other servants before they could sit down to eat. They had to show respect to their superiors.

DID YOU KNOW?

Baby boom
Victorian families were enormous! It was not unusual for parents to have nine or more children. That's a lot of people for a maid to clean up after!

Big Victorian **stately homes** employed at least fifty servants.

I thought helping around the house was tiring, but at least I've got machines like vacuum cleaners and dishwashers to help me!

BREAKFAST TIME

Big breakfast

By about 8 a.m., a maid could finally sit down to eat her own breakfast. Sometimes, she would have bread with cold meat left over from last night's dinner. If she was lucky, the cook would have prepared eggs and toast for all the servants, with a pot of tea. Breakfast was always a rushed meal – there was no time to stop and chat. Is breakfast like that in your home?

Serving breakfast was one of the busiest times in the day for a maid.

Dear Diary,
Disaster! Overslept this morning – got behind with chores. Housekeeper furious – banned me from breakfast in kitchen. Never liked her. Couldn't work on empty stomach … Cook took pity … gave me leftovers behind Housekeeper's back. Just in time, or I'd have fainted over Master's breakfast! Better not let this happen again, or I'm out of a job.

A Victorian breakfast was a very filling meal.

Good start

At 9 a.m., a maid would serve breakfast to the master and mistress in the breakfast room. Breakfast was an important meal for rich Victorians, with lots of choice on offer. A typical breakfast included jellied meat, cress and radishes, oysters, poached eggs, bread rolls and butter. All this, washed down with hot tea and fresh coffee. Do you eat this much before you go to school?

DID YOU KNOW?

Food frenzy

Wealthy Victorians liked their food! A hearty breakfast was followed by lunch at 1 p.m., afternoon tea at 4.30 p.m., then a massive evening dinner at 8 p.m. This was the largest meal of the day.

Say Your Prayers

Sunday best

A Victorian maid had to be religious. At about 8.30 a.m. every day, the servants said morning prayers together. The Christian religion was important to most Victorians; six out of ten people went to church every Sunday. Servants were supposed to go if they could spare the time, but they had to hurry back to work afterwards. Everyone wore their smartest clothes to church – they called this their 'Sunday best'. What do you usually do on Sunday, and what do you wear?

Women and girls wore hats to church.

Sunday fun day

In Victorian Britain, Sunday was a 'day of rest'. Maids were often given Sunday morning off to go to church and Sunday School. No shops were open on Sundays, and you couldn't play sport like you can today.

Children were not allowed to run, play games, or even read a book that had nothing to do with the Bible. They could only play with certain kinds of toys, such as a model of Noah's Ark.

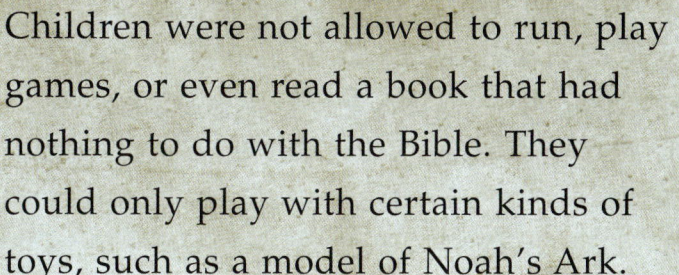

Lots of things were banned on Sundays back then. Thank goodness, things are different now.

Dear Mother,
I was given time off yesterday, so I went to Sunday School in the village hall. You always told me to go to school if I could, so I jumped at the chance. About a hundred children were packed into the hall. We started at 10 o'clock sharp and spent the next two hours practising our reading and listening to Bible stories. The teacher was a lady from church. She was very strict and kept us quiet!
Your loving
Hetty

Sunday Schools for poor children were also called **charity schools**.

Morning Slog

Take care

Do you sit down a lot at school? No such luck for a Victorian maid. Once she had tidied the breakfast things away, she would have to get on with more jobs. She would spend the morning filling oil lamps, scrubbing, cleaning and dusting. She would take care not to break anything, or she would have to pay for it out of her wages.

DID YOU KNOW?

Hands off!
A maid must not steal anything. She would instantly lose her job or be given a prison sentence. Theft was a serious crime. Some children who were caught were transported to Australia.

A maid had to be honest, or there would be trouble.

Girls versus boys

While the maid was working hard around the house, the master's children would be in the nursery, having lessons with a **governess**. Rich Victorian boys were treated differently from their sisters. At 8 years old, they were often sent away to boarding school, while their sisters stayed at home to learn music and sewing. Do you think this was fair?

Dear Mother,
I have been feeling most unwell. Housekeeper has let me off some of my chores, but she won't let me go back to bed. She says there is too much to do before the master's big dinner party tonight. I can't afford to see a doctor or buy medicine, but I'm afraid I will lose my position here if I don't get better very soon.
Your loving
Hetty

Wealthy parents paid a governess to teach their children at home.

GRAB LUNCH

Healthy diet?

What time do you have lunch? Maids would grab something to eat at midday, because they wouldn't have a chance to stop later. They would often eat leftovers and dip bread into beef fat, called dripping. Maids wouldn't have time to worry about a balanced diet, with plenty of fruit and vegetables.

THINK ABOUT IT!

REGULAR MENU

Imagine having the same meals every week. This would happen in many Victorian homes. For example, on Mondays, a cook might boil beef and bones. On Tuesdays, she would bake a pie, on Wednesdays, she might cook chicken, on Thursdays she may bake again and on Fridays, she would always cook fish. The vegetables would vary, depending on the time of year.

It was important to be nice to the cook as she was in charge of all the food!

Don't be late!

After finishing off her midday meal with a mug of tea, a maid would put the servants' lunch on the kitchen table. Then at 1 p.m. on the dot, she would serve the master's lunch in the dining room. Victorians liked to be on time, and the master would get angry if his meal was late. In summer, lunch was sometimes served outside in the garden.

The Victorians were keen on fresh air and would eat outside in good weather.

Dear Diary,
Lovely sunny day today. So warm, Master wanted luncheon outside, so we had to lay table and serve up in South Garden. Pleasant for him but hard work for everyone else!

Menu as follows:

Cold chicken
Boiled potatoes
Salad
Curried eggs
Veal cutlets
Bread and butter

For dessert:
Jam tart
Lemon custard

21

QUICK REST

Chilling out

In a Victorian house, lunch was usually cleared away by 3 p.m. After working for over nine hours, a maid could finally have a rest. When you have free time, perhaps you listen to music or chat to friends online? A maid might play a card game, write a letter or get on with some mending – if she didn't doze off first.

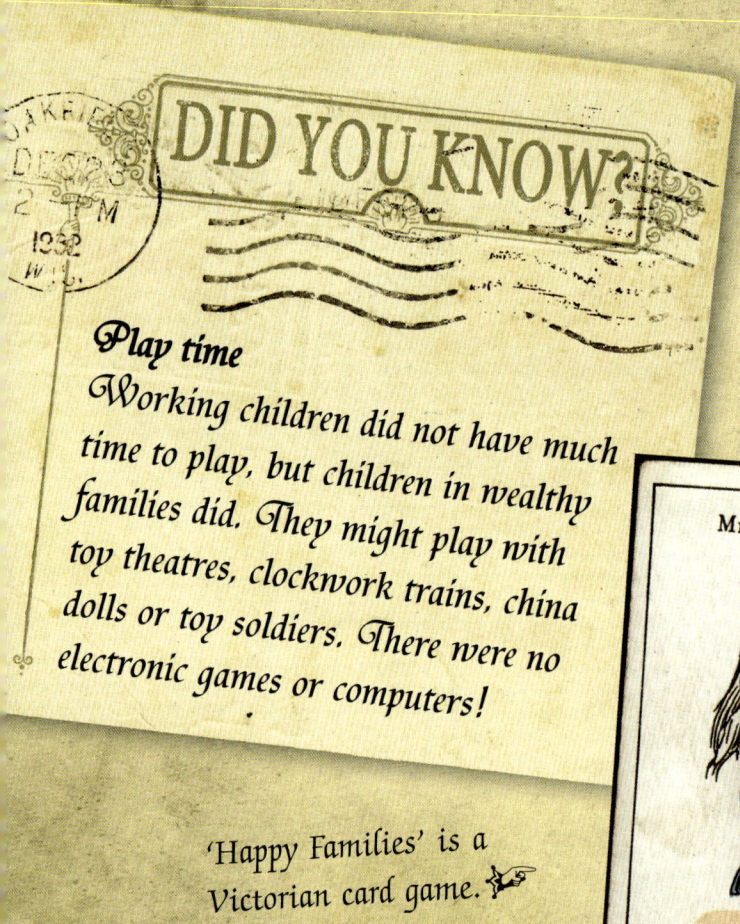

DID YOU KNOW?

Play time

Working children did not have much time to play, but children in wealthy families did. They might play with toy theatres, clockwork trains, china dolls or toy soldiers. There were no electronic games or computers!

'Happy Families' is a Victorian card game.

DID YOU KNOW?

Holiday time
Holidays became fashionable in Victorian times. Children from rich families would take a steam train to the seaside. But, like all working class children, a maid could not afford a holiday.

Dear Diary,
Went without break this p.m. Mistress rang bell wanting to use the telephone — amazing new invention. Saw her speak to friend who lives a mile away — didn't even get up from her chair! Invited friend for afternoon tea ... end result, more work for me in kitchen. Exhausted again, as usual.

I love hanging out with my mates! I wouldn't have time for that if I was a Victorian maid.

Afternoon tea
At 4.30 p.m., you've probably finished school and are starting to relax. At this time, a Victorian maid would be serving afternoon tea – a light meal of bread and cake which kept everyone going until dinner time. A maid would carry tea trays to the nursery and the drawing room, and then at 5.30 p.m., she would eat her own tea in the kitchen.

Dinner Party

Get set

Do you ever set the table for dinner at home? Be glad you're not a Victorian maid! At 6 p.m., a maid would have to start laying the table in the dining room. If there was going to be a dinner party, all the best china and cutlery would be on show. Victorian dinner parties had about twelve courses, so the maid had to put every single knife, fork and spoon in the right place.

Fun and games

Dinner party guests would arrive at 7.30 p.m. and would usually sit down to eat at 8 p.m. The children of the house would keep out of sight, upstairs in the nursery. They might play **parlour games** with their nanny, for example, an acting game called 'Charades', a game with a blindfold called 'Blindman's Bluff', or the old favourite, 'Pin the tail on the donkey'. They might also play board games, such as backgammon or chequers.

Adults also enjoyed playing parlour games, like chess, after dinner.

Time Out

Staying up

When guests left the dining room, a maid could clear the table. She would tidy up in the kitchen and, at about 11 p.m., she would stop for a simple supper of bread and cheese. The maid would be totally exhausted, but she couldn't go to bed until her master had turned in for the night.

THINK ABOUT IT!

GOING SOLO

Imagine being the only maid in the house. Middle class families who could only afford one maid employed a 'maid of all work'. This maid had to do all the jobs in the house, from cooking and serving to washing and cleaning.

A maid's life was very hard and lonely.

Ring me

As a maid waited to go to bed, she would pray that no more bells would ring for her that night. Bells rang in the kitchen if help was needed upstairs. There was a different bell for every room in the house, so a maid would know exactly where to go when a bell rang.

Bells were used to call servants.

Dear Mother,
Last night the dinner guests didn't leave until nearly midnight. By then, I'd been up for nineteen hours! I've only been in service for a week, but it feels like a lifetime. If I saved my wages for a year, I wouldn't have as much money as my lady spent today on a gift for her daughter. But I mustn't grumble. I'm lucky to work here, I suppose.
Your loving
Hetty

What a great idea! I wish we had bells in our house.

OFF TO BED

Sleep at last!

At about midnight, a maid would climb the stairs to her attic room. She would carry a candle, taking care not to trip and start a fire. It is much easier for you to creep about at night, because you can switch on a light! Before a maid went to bed, she might write a letter – she couldn't phone to keep in touch with her family. Finally, she would fall into bed. If she was lucky, she had a bed of her own, but if not, she might have to share her bed with another maid. She would snatch five hours sleep before she had to get up to start another day.

A maid wrote by candlelight, or by the light of a gas lamp.

I need my sleep! I don't think I would last five minutes as a Victorian maid.

THINK ABOUT IT!

JOB FOR LIFE

If you were a good maid and worked hard, you might get a promotion. A lady's maid could earn up to £60 a year! Girls who worked as servants were safe in their work most of the time but this wasn't true for children who worked in mills, factories or mines. Their jobs were often very dangerous.

A lady's maid had to be able to speak well, read, write and sew. She had to be honest, and she was not allowed to gossip with other servants.

Dear Mother,
I think I am doing a good job here. Today, Housekeeper told me she is very pleased with my work. Maybe one day, if I try hard enough, I'll become a lady's maid. Then I'll be able to buy you and Father some special presents!
Your loving
Hetty

Could you Survive as a Victorian Maid?

1 Do you like living with your parents?

A Not really. I'd rather be on my own.

B I love my parents but I like time by myself, too.

C I couldn't leave home. I'd miss my parents too much.

2 Do you like to get up early?

A Yes, I love getting started early every morning.

B I like a long lie-in at weekends, but I'm up early during the week.

C No, I'd rather stay in bed all day.

3 Do you try to look smart?

A Yes, I always look my best.

B I make an effort to look good for school, but that's all!

C I'm the world's scruffiest person.

4 Are you polite?

A Yes, I try not to be rude to anyone.

B I am polite, but only if people are nice to me.

C Why be polite when being rude is more fun?

5 Do you work hard?

A I don't stop until I've finished a job, however long it takes.

B I work hard, but I like to play, too.

C I'm laid back – I'd much rather relax!

6 Do you need time to chill out?

A No, I prefer to be busy.

B I have to rest if I'm tired.

C Yes, I need all the time I can get!

How did you score?

Mostly **A**s: Congratulations! You'd probably survive as a Victorian maid … you might even get a promotion one day.

Mostly **B**s: Could do better … You might have a few problems, but you'd probably hold onto the job.

Mostly **C**s: Bad luck! You probably wouldn't last a day in this job. You'd have to start looking for something else pretty soon!

Glossary and Index

antiseptic	chemical that kills germs
chamber pot	pot that is used as a toilet
charity schools	schools for poor children
governess	female teacher who gives lessons to rich children at home
housekeeper	chief servant
in service	working as a servant for a rich family
middle class	group between working and upper classes including teachers and doctors
omnibus	bus pulled by horses or powered by steam
parlour games	indoor games
privies	very basic outdoor toilets
sewage	human waste
stately homes	large, grand houses
transported	sent abroad to serve a prison sentence
upper class	richest and most powerful people
working class	people who do physical work for a living, such as servants or factory workers

---

afternoon teas 23
attic rooms 4, 28
bells 27
breakfasts 12, 14–15
chamber pots 5, 10, 11
charity schools 17
chimney sweeps 9
church and prayers 16
clothes 6–7, 16
dinner parties 24–25
factory workers 3, 9, 29

family size 13
family visits 5
food and meals 12, 13, 14, 15, 20–21, 23, 24–25
free time 16–17, 22–23
games and toys 17, 22, 24
governesses 19
holidays 23
inventions and discoveries 3
lady's maid 29
lunches 20–21

maid of all work 26
mine workers 3, 9, 29
nurseries 12, 19, 23
poor children 2, 3, 5, 7, 8–9
rich children 2, 7, 12, 19, 22, 23, 24
rules of behaviour 7, 13, 18, 25, 29
Sundays 16–17
toilets 11
Victoria, Queen 2